How to Control Your Anger

(Before It Controls You)

A Guide for Teenagers

Ron Potter-Efron

JOHNSON INSTITUTE®
Minneapolis

How to Control Your Anger
(Before It Controls You)

Johnson Institute
7205 Ohms Lane
Minneapolis, MN 55439-2159
(612) 831-1630 or 800-231-5165

ISBN 1-56246-025-0

Printed in the United States of America.

Contents

Introduction: Do I Have an Anger Problem?

"I blow up almost every day about something. My parents won't give me my freedom. School's a bore, and I hate the way they try to control me. My friends are great, but I even get into fights with them. Sometimes I feel like I'm going to explode."

Is this you? Do you scream and yell a lot? Hit or threaten to hit? Does your anger get you into trouble at school? Have you lost friends because they got tired of your arguing and complaining? Do you often fight with your brothers and sisters? Do you have an anger problem?

If you do, you should know that too much anger can really mess up your life. You could lose your best friends—after all, who wants to be around somebody who gets angry all the time? Constant complaining and arguing at home, school, or work will only get you in trouble. But most of all, it's not much fun to be angry. Even though fights might be exciting, in between the fights, life can get pretty crummy if you're angry most of the time.

Everyone gets angry from time to time. Normal anger can even be positive if it helps you get busy to make things better. Normal, healthy anger can lead to healthy action. Anger is healthy when:

- it stays anger and doesn't turn into aggression (physical attacks);

- you take responsibility for your feelings ("I'm angry," not "You make me mad.");

- it's about issues and not personalities ("I need the car tonight," not "You're the worst parents in the universe.");

- it only lasts a short time and doesn't grow into long-term resentments or grudges; and

- you can talk to those you are angry with without losing control (swearing, yelling, or saying things you later regret).

But anger isn't always good. Take the test below to see how much control you have over anger. Place a check in each space if the description fits you.

✔ **DESCRIPTION**

____ I often lose control of my anger.

____ I say or do things when I get mad that I later feel bad about.

____ I hang on to my anger for a long time—I won't or can't let go of it.

____ My parents or teachers say I have an anger problem.

____ My friends/boyfriends/girlfriends say I have an anger problem.

____ When I get mad I really want to hurt someone.

_____ I hit, shove, slap, pinch, or threaten when I get angry.

_____ It feels to me like I'm almost always angry about something.

_____ I try not to let my anger out, but then blow up anyway.

_____ I believe other people are the cause of most of my problems.

_____ Sometimes I can't stop arguing even when I want to.

_____ It seems like people are always picking on me.

_____ I say "I won't" or "You can't make me" a lot.

_____ I like scaring others by getting mad—that's how I get my way.

_____ My anger is "all or nothing." I'm either furious or calm; I'm never just a little angry.

_____ I've been suspended from school, lost jobs, been arrested, or gotten kicked out of my home because of my anger.

_____ I enjoy being angry—that's when I feel excited, strong, happy, tough, really alive.

_____ I argue with anybody in authority: teachers, parents, bosses, adults in general.

_____ I often try to make others angry—to stir things up.

_____ I often hate myself and do things that hurt me.

Count the number of items you checked and see where you fall in the ratings on the next page:

0-3 points.	Wow! Unless you haven't been honest with yourself, you probably have no problem with anger at all. Go through the list again just to make sure you're not denying reality.
4-6 points.	Not too bad, but you may have some stuff to work on.
7-9 points.	Danger. You probably have problems controlling your anger, but not all the time. It could get worse unless you're careful.
10-12 points.	Trouble. That's a lot of anger. Anger is definitely a real problem for you. Better get to work doing something about it.
13-15 points.	Big trouble. Anger is taking over your life. It's time to get serious about changing how you express your anger before it's too late.
16-20 points.	Disaster. Anger is wrecking your life. Almost everything you do is touched by your anger. Do you really want to live like this?

Here's another way to tell if you have an anger problem: You have an anger problem if your anger messes up any important area of your life, such as: friendships, family, dating, school, work, playing sports, health (such as hurting your hand by punching a wall), or driving.

Ever hear of the feelings bus? You are the driver of the bus and all your feelings are the riders—anger, sadness, fear, happiness, love, and even boredom ride along. If your anger starts driving the bus, you can expect a rough trip. Maybe you'd like to get off that bus for awhile or get back into the driver's seat. If so, keep reading.

Why Am I So Angry?

We have two facts now: 1) You are a teenager. 2) You have at least a "small" anger problem.

What's the connection? Well, actually there are many reasons why teenagers get caught up in being angry.

Common Reasons for Anger

Growing up in an angry family.

It's hard growing up in an angry family. When parents are angry a lot and don't know how to express their anger in a healthy way, kids don't learn how to handle their anger either. Dad may hit, threaten to hit, or just yell a lot—so might Mom, brothers or sisters, grandparents, uncles and aunts. In some families, just one person gets mad a lot, and everybody else lives on edge trying to keep the peace. In other families, everyone bullies each other, with no one listening to how others in the family feel. When it does get quiet in an angry family, the quiet doesn't last for long. Everything is seen as a problem, but none of the problems ever get settled.

People in angry families tend to look for reasons to get mad at each other. They are suspicious of one another, thinking of the rest of the family as opponents, not teammates or people they can count on.

Do you live in an angry family? Even if you do, you can still learn to be less angry. You can do it! But you'll need to talk with people outside your family—people your age and older who aren't always so angry. Look for role models of people who handle their emotions well. Ask them how they stay calm. Spend some time with their families if you can. That way you can learn how to handle your anger and talk with others about it without blowing up.

Nothing seems fair.

Maybe your dad said you could go to the party Friday night. Then he changed his mind—for no reason.

Or your mom promised to pay you for cleaning the house. You worked all morning. Then she says you shouldn't ask to get paid because everybody in the family has to help clean.

Mostly, it's adults who act unfairly. But you can't always trust your own friends either. They say they'll come over and don't. Or maybe they talk about you behind your back.

All this upsets you. People preach about honesty, then lie to your face. They lecture about trust and then break promises. They nag about responsibility, but forget their own duties. As you see it, the world may seem to be made up mostly of fakes, phonies, and cheats. Maybe you never noticed the unfairness when you were younger, but you sure do now. And you get angry when you think about it.

Adult responsibilities but no freedom.

George's parents are divorced. He's the oldest of three kids who live with their mom. Mom has to work, but the only job she could find is from 3 P.M. to 11 P.M.

George has to baby-sit after school. He doesn't get out often. His younger brother and sister resent that he is in charge. They won't listen or obey. Mom can't afford to pay him, either.

After awhile, George starts to feel cheated. Other kids his age have fun. They have time for themselves. He gets grumpy with his brother and sister. He fights with his mother all the time. He wants his freedom and he wants it now.

George isn't the only teenager who feels this way. Perhaps you also believe that you have too many duties and not enough freedom.

You want to make your own decisions.

For George, the problem is too much responsibility, but for other teenagers it's the opposite: They're not allowed to take on responsibility or make their own decisions. In short, they're treated like little kids.

Independence. That's what being a teenager is all about— becoming an adult and making up your own mind. So what happens when others try to tell you what to do, say, or think? Maybe that's when you get angry, even furious: "Let me live my own life! Let me make my own mistakes! I know what I'm doing! Back off!"

Your parents understand this need for independence sometimes, but they've got their own job to do. They're legally responsible for you until you're eighteen years old. Besides, they don't want to see you get hurt. So even the best parents can't give you total freedom.

Conflict between teens and parents is inevitable. Your job is to race toward freedom. Your parents' job is to keep you safe, to slow you down a bit. It helps a lot if you can understand each other. It helps if you can sit down together, talk, and try to find a compromise.

Runaway hormones, growth spurts, and sexuality.

It isn't easy being a teenager. All those hormones running through you and the changes your body is going through can make you irritated with yourself, other people, and the world around you. You might feel super happy one minute and depressed the next, and in between you might just feel irritated. Maybe you can't find clothes that fit right; or you have pimples; or you just feel dorky sometimes; or are afraid other people think you are. Maybe you get teased for things about your body that you have no control over, like your size or looks. All this is probably enough to make you angry, but on top of that you have a sex drive to deal with.

It's difficult to keep your mind cool when your body is hot. But that's exactly what teenagers have to do—especially teenagers who have problems with anger.

The sex drive is wonderful. It feels good. But that drive is also very demanding. It's easy to get mad at anybody or anything that gets in the way: worrying parents, boys or girls who don't want to go out with us; boyfriends or girlfriends who won't go all the way. Sexual frustrations can be awful. We have to be careful not to get angry, irritable, or even violent when we are frustrated like that.

One of the key elements in maturing as a person is learning how to be self-controlled in all circumstances. This process doesn't stop when you turn eighteen; it continues throughout your life. Sexual frustration is a difficult part of growing up, but something we all must face. Learning how to behave in a kind, appropriate way when you're sexually frustrated is difficult, but it can be done. It is also a foundational part of learning how to be in a loving relationship with someone else. We all have to learn to compromise and think of the other person's feelings and needs. Now is a good time to start.

Angry friends expect you to be angry, too.

Joseph and Maria are your new best friends. They are fun to be around. But, boy, are they angry. Joseph hates his parents. Maria hates the whole world. They expect you to be as angry as they are. Joseph wants you to fight with your parents and refuse to obey them. Maria wants you to badmouth all your other friends.

You want to keep these two as your friends, but beware! The cost may be great. Do you really want it to be "us against the world?" Do you want to stay as angry as they are? Remember that it's easier to become angry than it is to stop.

If you already have an anger problem, take a look at your best friends. They may be feeding your rage. You may be fueling theirs. Is that how you want to be?

Angry enemies.

Nobody, not even you, is liked by everybody. We all have people who don't like us much—enemies, rivals, those who belong to other groups, other gangs. When they are mad at you, you probably feel you are expected to be mad at them. Maybe you'd like to stop fighting, but think you can't because they would laugh at you.

You may find yourself trapped into being angry even though it isn't fun anymore. It isn't smart, either. But how can you get out of it if others are always challenging you to fight?

This is a hard one. Somehow you're going to have to find the courage to quit playing the tough guy—unless, of course, you want them to keep messing with your life so you can have a good excuse to stay angry.

Alcohol and other drugs.

Some people turn to alcohol or other drugs to escape from being angry and to help them feel better. This may work at first, but it doesn't take long before alcohol and other drugs eventually bring a person down, making the person feel even worse about himself or herself than when he or she first started using.

If you have an anger problem to begin with, alcohol or other drugs can lower your inhibitions. Inhibitions are those thoughts and feelings that keep you from doing things you might regret. Without them, you are that much more likely to do something out of anger that you'll get in trouble for or wish you'd never done. Maybe you will do something stupid at a party and feel embarrassed or guilty about it later. Then you get angry at yourself. If you drink again to get away from the anger or so you don't have to cope with your uncomfortable feelings, the same type of thing may happen again.

If you don't stop this cycle of using alcohol or other drugs early on, you may become chemically dependent. You may come to depend on alcohol or other drugs to help you escape all kinds of uncomfortable feelings.

The best way to stop alcohol or other drugs from making your anger problem worse is not to use them. Instead, work on the other things that are causing you to be so angry. If you're already having trouble controlling your urge to use alcohol or other drugs, speak to your parents, a high school counselor, or another adult you trust.

Pride and power.

Perhaps you're angry so often because it's something you're good at. You may not be great at math, or making friends, or making money, but you sure know how to get mad. You're proud of your ability to tick people off. Or maybe you get your own way by being angry—by screaming, yelling, threatening, hitting, or just plain being grouchy.

This is another reason for getting angry that's not easy to give up. But think about it. Is this the best way you can think of to get attention? Is this the only way to get what you want?

You feel bad about yourself.

Many teenagers have trouble with self-esteem. They look in the mirror and see ugly pimples. They aren't doing all that well in school. They can't count on their friends. They feel like they're on emotional roller-coasters. They say things like: "Nobody likes me. I don't fit in. I never will. I hate myself." Sound familiar?

Two things happen when you feel this way. First, you are angry with yourself a lot. You can't be your own best friend. You may even do things to hurt yourself or to ruin it when something good happens to you. The message to others is "Look at how much I hate myself. Just try to make me feel better."

Second, you may take your anger out on others. Instead of dealing with your own self-hatred, you try to push it onto someone else—"Hey, I'm O.K. It's you who stinks." That sneer in your voice, the look of disgust—maybe you can make others feel as bad as you do, or worse. Then at least you won't be alone in your misery.

What can you do to like yourself better? Self-acceptance is the key. You have to learn to accept yourself, even though you aren't perfect or as good as you'd like to be. Learning to like yourself may take some time, and you may need help from friends, family, and counselors. Try to be patient with yourself and others.

We've looked at some of the main reasons why teenagers get angry. How many fit your situation? You have the right to be angry about any or all of these things. But what good does it do you? How much anger can you afford? What are the costs?

Are you ready to consider becoming less angry? If so, read on.

What Can I Do to Control My Anger?

Be "selfish" about controlling your anger.

No matter who says you have an anger problem—your mother, father, teachers, friends, or counselors—the only one whose opinion really counts is you. Why? Because you won't change much until you decide that your anger is doing you more harm than good. Being selfish about controlling your anger means that you do it for yourself, so you can be happier and feel better.

Recovering alcoholics talk about getting "sick and tired of being sick and tired" before they were able to quit drinking. Are you "mad and angry about being mad and angry?" Have you had enough?

It's not easy to change the habit of being angry. You're going to have to think, talk, and act in new ways. Your family and friends may get in the way by expecting you to be angry just like you have been in the past. You may have to refuse to get angry despite their expectations.

You can choose to be angry or not to be angry. How do you know if it's time to stop being angry? Let's check it out.

First, make a list of the good stuff you gain by being angry, such as excitement, feeling powerful, getting what you want, people think you're tough, etc.

Now make a list of the costs of your anger—for example, troubles at home or school or with the law, lost friendships, headaches, endless arguments, lost privileges, driving tickets, accidents, fistfights, etc. Ask your friends for help with this list.

When you're done, compare your two lists. Think of the present—are you really happy with yourself this way? Think of the future—how angry do you plan to be next week, next month, or next year?

It's your choice. If you want to quit being so angry—or if you are still making up your mind—read on.

Take control of your anger.

Have you ever watched people point their fingers during arguments? "It's all your fault," they say. "You make me mad."

Forget it. If I have an anger problem, I'm the one making me angry, not them. Sure, other people do things I dislike. But so what? That's no big deal. It's me who won't take no for an answer or who won't stop fighting—I'm the one. I make myself angry.

You can't do anything about your anger until you take control of it. Good or bad, it's yours. Your anger starts in your mind, takes over your body, comes out your mouth.

If you refuse to take control of your anger, then others take over. Then your parents can make you mad any time they want—so can the teacher you don't like, your boyfriend or girlfriend, your kid sister or your older brother. In fact, unless you control your anger yourself, just about anybody can push your buttons and make you mad whenever they want. So who do you want in charge of your anger—them or you?

How do you start taking control? By telling yourself every day that you are in charge of your anger. Quit blaming others when you get mad. If you have to point a finger, turn it toward yourself. Let them know, "This is my anger, not yours. You can't make me get angry. You can't make me stop. I'm in charge. I'm in control."

Buy time.

To many teenagers, anger feels like a speeding car racing along almost out of control. The trouble is, we don't have time to react at that speed. Too often we crash and burn. When this happens, we're in a state of rage.

Anger + Going Too Fast = Rage

We can't always stop the anger, but we can stop the rage. The best way to stop anger from becoming rage is by buying time. Ever hear of a voluntary timeout? That's when you decide to get out of a situation before you do something bad.

Timeouts work like this: When you can tell you are about to explode or hit somebody, you GET OUT NOW. Not in five minutes. NOW. Before you explode, not after. Leave the room. Get away.

If you have to yell and scream, go outside or to your room. Either of these is better than yelling at someone who might yell back or hitting someone who might hit back, which would get you into more trouble.

Do something physical, like running or walking fast around the block. Go shoot baskets. Talk to a favorite teacher. Write a letter to a good friend. You might even ask your parents to get you some big foam blocks to keep in your room. Then when you're really mad and need to let it out, you can throw them at the walls without getting in trouble for breaking things or hurting someone.

Once you let off steam physically, do something relaxing, like reading a comic book or a story. Don't get on the phone and complain about how miserable everybody else is and how mad they make you. Remember, your anger is about you and not them. Stay in control of your anger.

After you calm down, go back and try to talk things out. Timeouts aren't the same as running away from an issue; they're a chance to cool off before you have to deal with it.

"Okay," you say, "I can do that. But what if some adult is giving me THE LECTURE? They're mad at me. They won't listen. And I can't leave. They insist I stand there and listen to them."

That's when you have to take an *inner timeout*. Only you know you're doing this. It happens inside you. You concentrate on taking one calm breath at a time. You tell yourself you're not going to let this person sucker you into exploding. You put up a mental wall. You listen just enough to get the message. You tune out the rest.

Stop the worst first.

Anger problems are like ladders that get taller with time. Over the years, or maybe months, you have built rungs onto the ladder. Each rung is something you do when you get angry. At the top of the ladder is the worst thing you do, with each rung below being not quite as bad as the one above. One teenager's ladder looked like this:

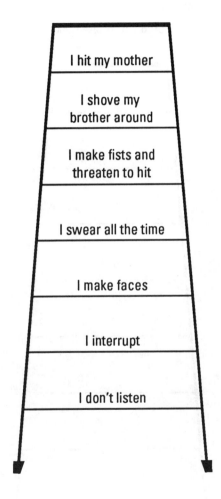

I hit my mother

I shove my
brother around

I make fists and
threaten to hit

I swear all the time

I make faces

I interrupt

I don't listen

The goal is to get off the ladder. The way to begin is by climbing down from the top.

Before we go on, would you please make your own ladder right here?

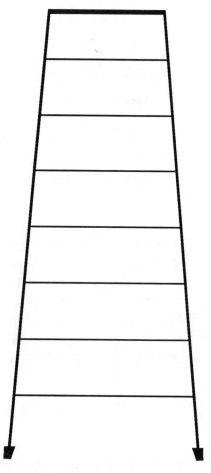

For now, let's just concentrate on the top rung. That's probably the one that gets you into the most trouble. If you could stop that one thing, life would get better. Make a promise to yourself to stop that one behavior—not that you will "try" to stop. Trying isn't enough. Doing is what counts. Fill in the following line.

Today, I promise myself that I will not _____

_____, no matter what.

Then make the same promise again tomorrow and the next day and the next.

Stop the worst first. Then start walking down the ladder. Maybe first you had to stop hitting. Now you've done that—no hitting for two weeks. What's next? Threatening? Swearing? Running away when you're angry and not coming back? Whatever it is, take the next step. You'll find each one a little easier to stop than the one before. Just keep walking down that ladder until you get off it completely.

Sort through your anger invitations— and throw some out.

It's been a busy day. You've received invitations to go to three different places tonight, but you only have time for one. What do you do? You pick one, and say "No thanks" to the rest.

Think of all the anger invitations you get every day: the alarm clock that wakes you up; your brother or sister hogging the bathroom; finding that you're out of orange juice or your favorite breakfast cereal; parents nagging about your homework; the bus coming early or late; the bus coming at all. And that's just the start of the morning.

An anger invitation is anything that you could choose to get angry over. But notice that word "choose." Angry people say "Yeah, sure" to a lot of anger invitations. So they're always mad about something. But for what? Who wants to be angry all the time?

You don't have to accept an anger invitation. You can say no. "No, thanks, I'm not going to let you bother me today." "No, thanks, I'll just have toast instead of cereal." "No, I choose not to get into that argument."

Figure that you'll get at least fifteen anger invitations today— fifteen chances to get upset. How many can you afford to accept?

Fishermen have a saying: SMART FISH DON'T BITE. You'll have to be a smart fish to get control of your anger. You don't have to take the bait just because it's out there.

Challenge your angry thoughts.

Sometimes it takes only one thought to send a person into anger. These are called trigger thoughts; they push on your anger button, triggering you to get mad. Trigger thoughts can also be "automatic" thoughts—sentences, phrases, or feelings we pull up out of habit, without thinking about it. When a trigger thought is also an automatic thought, we think that thought, and POOF, we're mad. Here are some examples of trigger thoughts:

- Nobody understands me.
- I hate _____(my parents, homework, cats, kissing relatives, etc.).

- They can't make me.
- They're out to get me.
- It's not fair.
- I want it NOW.
- They can't do that to me!
- I'm an angry person, and I always will be.
- I can't help it; they make me mad.

We each have our own trigger thoughts. Take a minute and write down three of yours.

My trigger thoughts:

1. _____

_____

2. _____

_____

3. _____

_____

Now's the time to regain control over your own brain. Here's how:

- First, identify your trigger thoughts. (You've already done that.)

- Next, cut them off. Take away their power. Stop them from controlling you.

- Third, switch to new thoughts. These new ones don't make you angry.

Here's an example of how it works: One of Ellen's trigger thoughts is "I never forget an insult!" A month ago, her best friend Sally got mad and called Ellen a name. Now Ellen's stuck. She can't forgive Sally. She can't forget. She won't talk with Sally. And she really misses her friend.

(1) What can Ellen do to get unstuck and be friends again with Sally? First, she needs to identify the trigger thought: "I never forget an insult."

(2) Next, she has to cut it off: "Look, this is stupid. I'm just hurting myself. I've painted myself into a corner. I want to be friends with Sally again."

(3) She has to switch to new thoughts: "I don't like being insulted, but it happens. I insult others sometimes. I can let it go after awhile."

Now Ellen is no longer stuck. She can talk with Sally. She can let go. She can be friends again.

Like we've been saying, it's up to you. You can keep your trigger thoughts and stay angry, or you can challenge them. You're in charge.

Put yourself in their shoes.

Lately, your best friend Ralph has been acting like an absolute idiot. He said he'd come over yesterday and then never showed up. So today he promises again. "I'll come by about 6 o'clock," he said.

And now it's 9 P.M. and he still hasn't shown up. Finally, you call him and he says he's sorry, but he's not coming over.

You're ready to strangle Ralph, aren't you? He has no right. . . .

And then he mentions that his parents are getting a divorce. And everything changes.

You're not mad at Ralph now. Instead, you know he's hurting. Maybe you remember a time when your parents separated, or when you thought they might. You can imagine how bad he feels. Now you're walking in Ralph's shoes.

It's hard to stay mad at someone when you walk in their shoes. But the time to do this is before you start yelling. That's when you can ask yourself these questions:

- What's he or she so upset about?

- Why is that so important to him or her?

- What is he or she feeling right now?

It's easiest to put yourself in the shoes of your best friends, so start with them. Then go on to your brothers and sisters, or others who are like you. Then try your parents or teachers or people who are very different from you.

By now you may be thinking, "WHO CARES WHAT THEY'RE FEELING?" Well, if you really want to be less angry, you should. You'll be less angry when you take the time to understand where other people are coming from.

Look under the covers.

Anger is a strong emotion; so strong it can even cover up other feelings, such as sadness, fear, and loneliness.

For example, you really want to do well this year in school, but you're having trouble in math. You just don't understand it. So you blow up in math class. You start throwing books around, swearing at the teacher, saying you won't study this stuff and no one can make you, that it's a waste of your time. Yes, you certainly are angry. But underneath the anger there are other feelings. What are they? Fear? Disappointment? Shame (feeling like there's something wrong with you)?

Here's another example. Your best friend is moving out of the neighborhood. You may never see her again. All of a sudden you are picking fights with your family. You're angry and frustrated that you have no control over the fact that your friend is moving. You're taking your anger out on your family instead of naming your *real* feelings: frustration, anger, sadness, loneliness, fear.

Anger is a feeling that hides other feelings. It's like a huge blanket that covers up all the others. It hides your real feelings from other people, but also from yourself. Sometimes, it's easier to be angry than to feel lonely, sad, or hurt. Sometimes it feels safer to be angry than to let people see your pain. Maybe you get angry to keep yourself from thinking about unpleasant or hurtful things, such as not making the basketball team, your parents' divorce, or your grandma's death. Perhaps you've gotten used to being angry—it's a habit. Or perhaps you told yourself you'd never cry and the only way you can stop is by getting really mad. Maybe people would care about you if you quit being angry all the time, and you're not sure you want to let them. Or maybe you live in an angry family where anger is the only feeling allowed.

Whatever your reason for using anger to hide your other feelings, you need to know that getting mad tells other people to keep away from you. Is that what you really want to say?

Try taking a peek under the covers. Find out what other feelings you have besides anger. Then start sharing those hidden feelings with others. Begin with the people you trust the most.

Then, when you start to get angry, ask yourself this one question: What else, besides anger, am I feeling right now? If you can take care of those other feelings, you won't have to get angry.

Practice fair fighting.

No matter how hard you try, sooner or later you're going to get angry about something and you'll want to let others know how you feel. Here is a list of "Do's and Don'ts" that can help you express your anger without making matters worse. *If you follow these rules you will probably get more of what you want.*

Don't

- hit, push, shove, hold, or threaten;
- stand up and yell;
- make faces or make fun of others;
- swear or call people names;

- get stuck in the past;

- say "Forget it," "Tough," "Who cares," "So what," etc;
- say "always" or "never";

- interrupt;

- always have to get the last word;
- have to win every battle.

Do

- sit down and talk;

- stick to one issue at a time;
- take timeouts before you lose control;
- listen—really listen—to what the other person is saying;
- slow yourself down—breathe calmly, relax;
- attack problems, not people;
- be open to discussion, bargaining, compromise;
- be flexible—able to change your mind if you want;
- be responsible for what you say and do;
- state your feelings.

Most of the "don'ts" are pretty clear. Hitting, swearing, yelling, name-calling, making faces, interrupting—all this stuff makes situations worse instead of better. So does saying things like "Tough," "Who cares?," "You always do that," or "You never do this." Sure, all these things let people know you're angry, but that's all they're good for. You won't get what you want by acting that way.

It also doesn't do you any good to get stuck in the past. Let go of your old resentments and start over with people. Hanging on turns anger into hate.

Don't try to get in the last word or win every battle. When you do that, you're just arguing for the sake of arguing. Then others do the same and nothing gets done.

The "do's" are important. They turn arguments into discussions, no-win situations into both-win situations. We've mentioned some of them before: taking timeouts, slowing down, listening, stating your feelings, taking responsibility for your own actions (not making excuses). Let's look at some of the others.

First, stick to one issue at a time. If you're trying to defend your right to drive the car while your parents are trying to talk with you about your grades, neither one of you will get anywhere. You won't get the car. Your parents won't get through to you about your grades. First find a solution to one issue, then work on the next.

Second, it's okay to argue about an issue, but it's not okay to attack people. Keep to the topic. One "Oh, yeah? Well, your brain is fried, you stupid moron" leads to another. You may end up on top with the insults, but you probably won't convince the person you're arguing with that you're right about the issue.

Finally, be open to discussion, bargaining, and compromise. Be flexible. The goal is to solve the problem that triggered your anger. Look for new ways to think about the subject. Be creative.

Nobody can make you follow these "do's" and "don'ts." It's entirely your choice. But if you want to use your anger well—if you want to solve your problems instead of making them worse—then these rules can help you get what you want.

Conclusion

It's not much fun being angry a lot. In fact, anger is really a pretty lousy feeling most of the time. Who would choose to be angry when they could be happy instead?

Here's a chance for you to decide to be less angry. As you see, there's plenty you can do to become less angry. Once you have it under control, you can even use your anger to help you solve your problems.

It's your anger. It's your life.

It's your choice.